PINPRICKS

poems

PINPRICKS

poems

ANKIT RAJ OJHA

Hawakal
PUBLISHERS
New Delhi | Calcutta

HAWAKAL PUBLISHERS PRIVATE LIMITED
70 B/9 Amritpuri, East of Kailash, New Delhi 65
33/1/2 K B Sarani, Mall Road, Calcutta 80

Email info@hawakal.com
Website www.hawakal.com

Cover designed by Bitan Chakraborty

First edition (paperback) July 2022

ISBN: 978-93-91431-16-7 (paperback)

Price: INR 150 | USD 11.99

For *Baba* and *Maaji*

FOREWORD

My trek on Twitter and Instagram began this year in mid-January. In the initial phase of my foray, I chanced upon Ankit Raj Ojha, and soon *we followed each other*. This kept me abreast of his poems published in this or that journal. I noticed his interactions with others from the community. He had the makings and markings of a literary citizen, positive comment to one, an emotional nudge to another.

When the Mentor Chapbook series offer dropped by from Hawakal, I sought Ankit's manuscript. Reading *Pinpricks* has been a rewarding experience. Ankit has quiet humor. His lines flirt with the mirthful, but behind his jocular moorings lies a mind searching for soothers. His poetic gaze permeates the textures of his milieu: this ensues fine observations. I'm sure you will enjoy his poems as much as I did.

I wish Ankit Raj Ojha all the best with his career as an author. Peruse his writings at your will.

Sanjeev Sethi
June 2022
Mumbai

ACKNOWLEDGEMENTS

I express my greatest debt to my father, Prof. Uday Shankar Ojha, for introducing me to literature at an age when all I was supposed to do was eat clay and play in puddles of mud until thrashed and dragged back into our home (I *did* do all of that, in addition to watching my father teach his students). I love my mother, Smt. Kiran Ojha, for being my first *guru* who taught me to read and write before I was ready for school and whose constant nagging about my faulty pronunciation corrected my mother tongue. I can never thank my brother Anand enough for supplying me with an endless stock of his wicked sense of humour, wit and observation which I try my best to toy with in my literary experiments. I am immensely grateful to my uncle, Shri Mani Shankar Ojha, for staying awake on innumerable nights playing songs to a little me and stuffing my pea-sized brain with the beauty of metre and rhyme. I thank my aunt, Smt. Sunaina Ojha, and my sister and brother, Nancy and Ankur, for they are the best family I could ask for.

I am eternally grateful to Smt. Sabitri Pradhan, my mother-in-law, Shri Rabinarayan Dhal, my father-in-law, and Dr. Bhabani Sankar Dhal, my brother-in-law, for being the sweetest and most supportive "in-laws."

Words fail me as I thank my *guruji* Prof. Nagendra Kumar, *guru-maa* Smt. Kalindi Chaturvedi, Ananya, Kushagra and Percy for giving me the most loving family away from home. I also thank my friends and the wonderful people I know from my hometown Chapra, Bokaro, Delhi NCR, Infosys Mysore, Infosys Bhubaneswar, IIT Roorkee and Haryana for their immense support.

This book has been made possible largely due to the kind guidance of Mr. Sanjeev Sethi, an amazing poet and an even amazing human being, who *found* me, honed me and made this happen. I am grateful to Dr. Kiriti Sengupta and Shri Bitan Chakraborty at Hawakal for giving me the bragging rights of having a poetry collection to my name.

As I sit down to write this, I feel the loving presence and blessings of my dearly departed grandparents, Smt. Sumitra Devi and Dr. Madan Mohan Ojha, who gave me the life they never had.

I have saved my wife, Biswamohini Dhal, for the last because I know that when all is gone, she will be there with me till the end of the line. *Thank you for everything, my girl. I mean it!*

CONTENTS

PALATE

I told my grandpa
I'd send him kimia dates—
the ones they don't have
in our hometown.

He was thrilled,
lifelong lover of the Iranian import
who had never tasted beyond
cheap local rip-offs,
but dismissed me
for they-must-be-expensive!

I had a box lying around
but decided to get him another
when I'd be done revising
my paper.

He showed symptoms on May 2nd,
was dead on the 13th.

I have a boxful
of original kimia dates
and a paper in Routledge.

THE BOY NEXT DOOR

It is diwali night and this year too
my job has kept me from visiting
home for the festivities,
adding another to my ever growing
list of diwalis away from home.

So I put up my indifferent façade and treat myself
to *tandoori aloo paratha* and *dahi* at a *dhaba*
and have just returned to my residential society when
the aunty next door calls on me to join
the celebration on the rooftop followed by dinner.
And I join, despite myself, getting
to know my neighbours for the first time,
playing with their kids, dusting
firecracker ash from my sleeves and
the inevitable ache
of being called "uncle" by the brats.

When dinner arrives I have a heartful,
my neighbours never suspecting how
the boy next door has
smiled his way through his
second dinner of the evening.

First published in *The Dillydoun Review* (Issue 14).

GENERATION GAP

Like my father, I too am
a man of literature.
Last night while watching
Ustad Shafqat Ali Khan play
roller coaster with his vocal tract
in concert, Papa said
that the ustad's voice flows
like a clear stream through
a meadow.
I was itching to offer
a simile of my own
featuring quite another tract,
and diarrhoea,
but then I chose to shut up.

First published in *Roi Fainéant Press* (March 20, 2022).

FOR PAPA

It is not easy
to let your guard down,
iron the brow,
the indelible frown—
a vile reminder
of being a man.

PORTRAIT OF A LADY TAKEN TOO SOON

Last night I came across
a photograph of my grandma
in an old smartphone;
a picture of a photograph,
twice removed from reality.

I touched to scroll away
and my thumb didn't lift.
Despite the seventy one kilos of my prime,
I was arrested by the old woman's glare.
I tried looking away, yet looked hard
at the creased maze
with its twin portals leading
to my past,
and ghosts of days gone by materialized,
flooding my throat
like bile rising up an abused stomach,
gagging me
with memories of my treachery.
The weary twists and turns
of her yellowed broken skin
seemed worthier
and farther
than the highway to the office.

I gazed and gazed
and all I had conquered was vain.

Broken, battered,
my pride shattered.

One point five millimeters of tempered glass
was an ocean.

First published in *Brave Voices Magazine* (February 9, 2022).

CAVITIES

An inscrutable joy rushes in
every time I chance upon
an empty cabinet,
an unused drawer,
or tight-lipped cavities
hitherto undiscovered
in rented apartments
I move in from time to time.

The sweeter the joy
if the compartment is empty
and struggles before giving in
to endless space
and infinite possibilities
tamed within tangible boundaries
erected to ease the insecurity
we hold against voids limitless
and unfathomable.

Cavities console us,
despite our wariness,
for things only dilute;
empty spaces hold infinity
within their walls.

Cavities are our
partners in crime,

where we lead
secret lives,
where we tuck
our truest selves
for safekeeping.

First published in *A Thin Slice of Anxiety* (March 15, 2022).

THE MAN WHO APPROPRIATED DEATH TO MY CONVENIENCE

He would sit alone outside,
my grandfather in his plastic chair,
gazing at passersby—
cows, women, dogs, men, goats, buffaloes, children
—for hours on end, alone,
save for the occasional company
of some *mohalla* friend of his—
Tantan chacha or *bank waale sahab*, usually.

He had this thing we often complained about.
He would call us from the ground floor
(he had moved to the room downstairs ever since
the man on the motorbike had hit his bicycle,
giving him sciatica for life),
in a volume and tone that
screamed "urgent" in all-caps,
bold and underlined,
and would not relent until one or all
of us would be assembled in his court;
then he'd say he forgot what it was,
or that maybe he'd tell it later,
or would utter something trivial that
would frustrate us to the core.

He would never trouble *me* for anything,
knowing I would be studying.

My mother, father and brother were his only
go-to for the needs and whims of his age,
agitated on the days when his scheduled 4 pm visit
to the homeopathic drug store would be
the only thing talked about in the house since morning.

I had always dreaded the inevitable,
failing to fathom how I would hold myself in the event.

Death calms, they say,
kills the element of surprise
and spontaneity of grief reserved
for some unseen and fearfully anticipated point in time.

Death too he took care of on his own,
ensuring I was not disturbed till the very end,
my brother and father being failed superheroes,
I crying uselessly on video call
a thousand miles away.

ESSENTIAL SERVICES

My cousin, the know-it-all procrastinator,
would rather host *litti chokha* barbecues in his backyard
than sit at the shop his father bleeds his pension for.

My uncle, tomorrow-man's father,
plays cards with his gang in the alley all day
for there's no social distancing at the office.

The socially distanced animal's brother,
l'homme de la littérature,
has cancelled his gym membership
(*one must not work out masked!*)
and has long unmasked dinner chats
with the pretty lady down the street.

The immunity conscious pretty lady,
doctor's wife and too good for our town,
nibbles on *sushi* and stuffs her enamoured husband
with last night's leftover *seekh kebabs*.

The French littérateur's woman,
president of Gossipers Anonymous,
holds the weight-watcher's witch trials at her place
to avoid the evening rush at the vegetable market.

The diabetic doctor, husband of the alleged witch,
sermons at-risk gluttons on weekdays
and on weekends attacks the crowded corner bakery

armed with insulin jabs.

The baker's wife who'd rather keep
her twelve children out of school than risk infection,
crams them in the lorry headed for the market
for she needs no less than
the baker's dozen to carry her ingredients.

The lorry driver who won't wear a mask for
how-on-earth-would-he-chew-tobacco-in-one,
forbids his wife from visiting Gossipers Anonymous hotspots.

The lorry driver's wife,
sulking at her overanxious tobacco-chewer,
vents out by inviting her aunts and sisters from across town
for risk-free lunch at her home.

One of her sisters,
nurse and my mother's friend,
gladly accepts mother's invitation
to bring her kin over for dinner at our place.

My mother, furious at my precautionist father
who didn't take her out shopping
and went to play cards himself,
insists that I bring my band
for an acoustic set at the ladies' dinner.

I, fully aware that gatherings
must be avoided for the good of all,
am slipping out at dusk
to have my poem peer-reviewed
at my know-it-all cousin's barbecue.

First published in *Roi Fainéant Press* (February 6, 2022).

CIRCLE

I am a circle of my own making,
drawing myself round and round
a centre I have tethered myself to,
a centre that houses
the what-ifs and so-whats
that wound and nurse my pride.

I keep waiting for a miracle,
a nudge from without
that'll free Sisyphus.
Then I'll be a tangent leaving its locus,
never to be drawn back
in its godforsaken orbit.

First published in *A Thin Slice of Anxiety* (March 15, 2022).

SUPPOSEDLY STOLEN LIVES

I often wonder if I could flip
the pages back to the time
free of constant fretting
over where I'm headed.

And in yearning to restore
what is long gone,
I tend to do stuff I did back then—
lying with a paperback
and a song on retro radio,
or strumming a Kishore Kumar melody
'till the blues go away—
all vain efforts at recreating
what time has stolen from me.

I have realized lately
in these designs of mine:
if we are so capable
of taking frequent detours
to our beloved past,
doing all we could
in the days of our lives
(days rendered spotless by bias and time),
aping every memory worth pining for again
(barring the few beyond resurrection)—
are we really as wretched
as we pride ourselves in believing?

First published in *A Thin Slice of Anxiety* (March 15, 2022).

PRIDE

Pride
breeds on
a steady source
of income.

First published in *Streetcake Magazine* (Issue 77, Part 2).

EMI

I am spending
myself
in installments.

First published in *Roi Fainéant Press* (February 13, 2022).

DINNER

Dinner
tastes better
than philosophy.

First published in *Roi Fainéant Press* (January 30, 2022).

NO, THANKS!

They show me a ghastly mirror—
a dwindling reflection
from a distant day ahead
when I am rendered useless
for lack of trying,
apparently.

They examine my heart,
feeling for fault lines
and feelings at fault,
then bring the axe down,
swinging *sans merci*
'till cracks appear.

But what if I break the jinx?
What if I refuse to age?
Let us say that I plant my blatant denial
to listen to the cautionary tale.
I shall have all the time in the world
to chase my muse, sweetly,
at my own pace.

First published in *Trouvaille Review* (January 11, 2022).

THE BARREL

Two men stand terrified
on either side of
the barrel—
one praying for life,
the other
for the afterlife.

A DOG'S LIFE

I see Mangi in our street every day,
lonely old drunkard who at a hat's drop
invokes god and serves the choicest abuses
in delicious Punjabi.

They say he comes from money,
that his father was high up in the government,
that he himself held a government job,
that his wife cuckolded and left him
for another man,
that his brother died
leaving him their ancestral six-bedroom house
with a garden and a lawn and a car-stuffed garage—
all at his disposal to dispose off.

Mangi lives alone in the house that once was
the neighbourhood's envy and now looks like
something Edgar Allan Poe would have
dreamt into life.
It is the street bitch's favourite haunt to lay her
sets of bastards in succession
and raise them on Mangi's property until they are
old enough to lead their own doggy lives
or die dogs' deaths between tyre and asphalt.

Mangi is Boo Radley except he comes out.
He eats at the *gurdwara* as no other

porch in town would have him.
You can see him roaming the street anytime,
day or night,
teaching manners and religion to teenage girls who
get picked and dropped by
a slideshow of boyfriends,
getting filmed by kids who hit the cricket ball
at him to trigger a train of educational expletives
vital for their rite of passage,
cursing and pampering street dogs who pay no heed
as if they knew he's one of them—
wretched, stinking, unwanted, harmless,
one-man-carnival for the whole neighbourhood.

THE LIFE AND TIMES OF SUKU AND DUKHU

Once upon a time in a village by the river
lived Suku and Dukhu, sister and brother.
Suku and Dukhu wasn't their real name.
It was their father's loving call,
which they grumbled was lame.

She played ludo in the tree and dipped in the pool,
little Suku wore her brother's shirt to school.
Mother packed them fish-rice and a pickle of lime,
and sent the kids off with a bottle and a dime.

Seasons came, seasons were gone
and many a trendy dress she wore.
But grown up Suku could love none
the way her brother's baggy shirt she'd adore.
She did well, went to the fashion college in town.
And oft she wondered how to make a pretty gown.

She went on tweaking until the day it dawned—
the key was the village by the river
that held her memories fond.
My childhood memories I'll weave on my gown!
Suku lit up as a smile soothed her frown.

Loose baggy silhouettes she made,
cut in her notebook's geometric shape.

She styled her dresses with badges and ties,
drawing from her childhood
as she wondered how time flies.

Checks and stripes she borrowed from her brother,
thought long and deep to match one with the other.
Here and there she put some ruffles,
to keep it together she made fabric buckles.

She coloured her dresses in memories of yore,
going back in time as they flashed and wore.
Some came off vague, some were fresh,
hence the black and white, and ludo colours in her dress.

She styled her dresses, tried with a pony and a bun,
until it was fit for any woman.
And thus with much work and fun,
Suku stitched her Spring Summer Collection.

Note: I wrote this piece as a fun experiment while watching my fashion designer wife fret for weeks on end over her college design project (we were dating at that time). I took it upon myself to calm her. We travelled places, met artisans and craftsmen looking for inspiration, until she found her project idea in her childhood. I have deliberately used a childish voice and amateur rhyme as an homage to every creative person out there who has managed to keep the child in them alive. Hold on. Did I tell you that she went on to win the Best Design Collection that year? She read this poem to the jury when asked to explain her project which happens to have the same name.

First published in *Roi Fainéant Press* (April 3, 2022).

MAHANADI

If only I knew I was marrying a baby!
She taunts me, laughing as she gets in
the front seat of her father's Honda Activa,
signalling at me to hop on the back seat.

I don't know how to ride a two-wheeler.
I have been too busy studying, watching
superhero cinema, playing gigs with my band,
fending off my inevitable male-pattern baldness—
a gift from my father's side.

I have managed to retain my apical pride all the way
into my third decade, beating Papa's and Baba's genes
so far, but have missed out on knowing how it feels
to be sitting in the driver's seat of a motorcycle—
the mundane thrill of feeling a rush of air
coursing through the vegetation on the head
is an adventure to me.

This morning in Cuttack is no different as I sit on
the back seat feeling second-hand wind kissing
the Mahanadi and in turn rustling my hair that have
long outstayed their welcome.

She parks at a petrol pump and senses instantly my
unease at stopping in a remote spot amidst
rough-looking men.

She puts me at ease, saying there's nothing to worry,
for this is Odisha, her home turf, where they have
a festival to worship menstruating women, and where
most men are dark only in skin.

We resume with a full tank, the riverside road stretching
forever with the Mahanadi, like the Mahanadi.
The trees are the deepest shade of green, appearing
almost fake as if painted twice over.

We stop for coconut water. The *nariyal waala* cracks open
sunroofs in two coconuts in less than half a dozen strikes,
puts in straws and we're good to go.

I follow her up a small flight of stairs onto a river view point
peppered with shy married couples
and brazen unmarried ones.

As I gaze in awe at the sprawling blue waters
(blue to the point of disbelief)
and try in vain to hide my hair in a bandana
from the damp river wind, she recounts simpler days
from her childhood, of how on Sunday mornings her father
would take her to buy fresh handpicked fish and prawns
from the riverside, and how their pampered cow named *Cow*
would run the entire household.

The choicest dairy products,
milk for the fish in the pond to grow fat on,
manure from cow dung,
cow dung cakes for cooking fuel,
biogas to power the home and the vehicles, and more.
Maybe *this* is why they call an *animal*
Mother, not for some mythic magic tale.

I listen intently, growing content at how she relishes
the tales featuring fish and crabs and prawns
and her grandma's cooking pot.
I am a vegetarian yet I do not flinch at her graphic description.
We have an understanding.
She'll never ask me to eat meat, and I'll never keep her
from her native food preference.

Fearing that her tales must have made me suffer,
she drives us to a vegetarian tiffin point by the river.
The pot-bellied shop owner is amused at my broken Odia
and asks her if I am not from around here.
She tells him I'm from Bihar and he is delighted,
recounting his time as a soldier stationed in my home state
and quickly unloading on our plate another serving
of hot spicy *ghughuni* despite our protests.

The bill comes to 25 rupees, nothing compared to what
I am used to spending on a decent breakfast in the north.
I almost feel bad for the ex-soldier who sells food this good
this cheap, and am instantly overcome with shame at
having allowed the patronizing thought to creep in.

She is about to hit ignition when she is distracted by
a cow mooing beside her and a dog tugging at her feet.
She descends as if to greet and reunite
with a long forgotten memory.

The dog gobbles a dozen *idlis,* the cow four times that much.
We ride back home on the dreamy Mahanadi road,
she transported to her history, I smiling ear to ear
at having spent way more than what I usually do on breakfast.

ON LOVE

The stupidest tragedy
is when a *ghat* longs
to own a river that at best
can serve its apportioned share
before meandering detached
on her majestic journey.

Has a river ever stopped
to pour all of herself
to a bleeding *ghat*?

I FREQUENT THE LESS FREQUENTED BOOKSHOPS

I frequent the less frequented bookshops,
blushing with the humility of a less than
bestselling author whose books rest
content behind bestseller rows.

The staff do not notice my unremarkable air
until I, shyly, introduce myself.

They take me in with awe,
making me comfortable in their best chair,
huddling around as if I were the
Neil Gaiman or Stephen King of India
(though I doubt that they've heard of them).

I insist against the special treatment,
clarifying that I am but a humble penman
whose author photo doesn't even
make it to his book sleeves.

They get me their best coffee,
sometimes a snack too to clog it down with,
for they are but a less frequented bookshop
eager to pamper the hell out of any
celebrity who strolls in their front door
mistaking them for an eminent establishment.

Once seated and stuffed, I get to sign
author copies of my minor modern classics—
a dream I have nursed all my life.

The few customers stare puzzled, unable
to place my face among the authors they read.
One or two buy signed copies,
more for their Instagram stories
than out of genuine interest in my work,
though I shy away from their cameras,
making up for it with sweet personalized notes.

On those rare rewarding occasions,
some fan engages me in an animated chat
on how they loved it when she dumped
that idiot to be with the one who
saw her for who she was,
or how they absolutely hated me for
killing off the star-crossed lovers;
to which I offer my earnest apologies
and explain how it was the only way
the story held itself together.

Once the heat has died, the bestsellers
are cleared to put my signed copies up front.
It's the least the bookshop can do for
the only celebrity who would ever
walk inside their humble establishment.

A few more autographs later,
I take leave of my gracious hosts
and come home content,
having lived my lifelong dream
yet again.

I am camera shy.
I am a ghost on the internet.
My books make it only so far as the
bookshops with no social media presence.
I am a writer who has never
written a book in his life.
So I frequent the less frequented bookshops.

ENDLESS PICARESQUE

Hometowns are inadvertent;
everything after that
a conscious effort
to keep yourself
thinkingly occupied
for life.

GLOSSARY

kimia dates — a variety of dates native to Iran

tandoori — a style of cooking in the Indian subcontinent and Middle Asia based on the use of a *tandoor* (clay oven)

aloo paratha — a popular Indian flatbread stuffed with spiced potato mixture

dahi — Hindi for "curd"

dhaba — a roadside eatery typically located on Indian highways and serving local cuisine

mohalla — a street, neighbourhood or community in a town or village in the Indian subcontinent

chacha — the Hindi/Urdu word for "uncle"

bank waale sahab — Hindi for "the gentleman who works at the bank"

litti chokha — a popular vegetarian dish from the Indian states of Bihar, Jharkhand and Uttar Pradesh. *Litti* is a baked wheat ball stuffed with spiced *sattu* (Bengal gram flour) and *chokha* is a spiced mixture of roasted and mashed brinjals, potatoes and tomatoes.

l'homme de la littérature — French for "the man of literature"

sushi — a Japanese dish typically prepared with sticky rice and some type of fish or seafood rolled and steamed together

seekh kebab — a type of *kebab* made by assembling spiced minced meat on skewers and cooking on a barbecue or a *tandoor*

sans merci — French for "without mercy"

gurdwara — a place of assembly and worship for Sikhs, where people from all faiths are welcomed and served free meals

Mahanadi — Sanskrit for "great river". It is a major river in East Central India flowing through the states of Chhattisgarh and Odisha.

nariyal waala — Hindi for "coconut seller"

ghughuni — a curry made of peas, chickpeas or Bengal gram, common to the Eastern Indian states of Bihar, Jharkhand, West Bengal and Odisha among others

idli — a savoury rice cake originating in Southern India and Sri Lanka, made by steaming a fermented batter of rice and black lentils

ghat — a broad flight of steps or a passage leading down to the bank of a river in India. For centuries, *ghats* have been in use for bathing, cremating the dead and for other Hindu rituals.

www.ingramcontent.com/pod-product-compliance
Lightning Source LLC
LaVergne TN
LVHW040928150826
845672LV00007B/2250

* 9 7 8 9 3 9 1 4 3 1 1 6 7 *